T
Guide to Handling Ohio Accident Claims

2023 Edition

By Attorney David M. Chester
The Chester Law Group Co., LPA

Helping Those Injured in Ohio

Recover from

Motor Vehicle Accidents

The Insider's Guide to
Handling Ohio Accident Claims

By Attorney David M. Chester
The Chester Law Group Co., LPA

*Helping Those Injured in Ohio Recover
from Motor Vehicle Accidents*

The Chester Law Group Co., LPA
430 White Pond Drive   Akron, Ohio 44320
1-800-218-4243
www.chesterlaw.com   info@chesterlaw.com

Contents

1

Foreword

Thank you for requesting this book. If you are like most people who have been involved in an accident you probably have a lot of questions. I wrote this book to help answer those questions and give some guidance through the difficult process of handling your injury claim. Let's face it; whether you are dealing with a catastrophic slip and fall injury, serious motor vehicle accident, injury on someone's property at an amusement park, or injury by a medical professional, the insurance companies that represent the person at fault that you will be dealing with are professionals at the personal injury game. Most of the time their interests are different than yours and that can put you at a disadvantage. I am here to help even the playing field.

My name is David M. Chester and I am an Ohio personal injury lawyer. Obtaining justice for my injured clients has been my life's work. As a child I was involved in an auto accident and my claim was not handled properly. As a result I still have health problems from that accident. I do not want this to happen to you or someone you love. To avoid this, I want to provide you with information about what happens when someone is injured in a car accident, the tricks and tips you need to know so you can make informed decisions about your injury claim.

Now throughout this book you will see me talking about insurance company adjusters making offers, negotiating, playing hardball, etc. You will not find me talking much about the role the party at fault plays in the personal injury process. This is because they actually play a very small role in the process. Their insurance company takes over the role of negotiator, and actually keeps their at fault insured out of the process for the most part. At most, my clients may see the party at fault if the case goes to litigation. Other than that, the battle is fought against the insurance company that represents the party at fault. And trust me, they are a well-trained, formidable, powerful opponent.

Over the last few years, in the case of motor vehicle accidents, for example, we have seen the auto insurance companies move away from making large early offers to injured victims to keep lawyers out of the process, in general. We are now seeing more low offers across the board, forcing people to either accept what we consider unreasonable offers or hire a lawyer and wait for a fair settlement. As we say in the personal injury profession, insurance companies will pay you quickly or fairly, but not both. In other words, if you want a generous settlement, you will have to jump through some legal hoops which probably will require an experienced Ohio

personal injury lawyer.

In reality, the days of handling things yourself and getting an appropriate settlement that takes care of all your future medical needs, protects your medical benefits and adequately compensates you for your injuries are quickly coming to an end. To be blunt, in my experience, insurance companies only understand force and the risk it brings to their bottom line, and what force does a non-lawyer really have against the multi-billion dollar insurance companies. It is like David fighting Goliath without any stones to throw.

A competent, aggressive personal injury lawyer is the stone you can use to hurt the insurance company in the only place that counts, their pocket book. You would not do brain surgery on yourself, but I am surprised by how many hard working, honest Ohioans do not realize the complexities of personal injury law including:

- The make whole doctrine
- Breach of subrogation clauses
- Indemnification and duty to defend clauses
- Robinson v Bates and subrogated carrier evidentiary issues
- Non-duplication clauses
- Liens/assignments and Letters of Protection and how they affect case value
- UCR and evidentiary rules regarding medical bill reasonableness and admissibility
- Pro-rating of prior and subsequent injuries
- Loss of enjoyment of life rankings
- Permanent impairment ratings - who can give them and how they increase case value
- Duties under duress and how it affects the case value
- Colossus and other insurance computer claim evaluation programs
- Medicare and Medicaid repayment rules and penalties for non-repayment
- How to avoid loss of health benefits upon settlement of the injury claim

Just to name a few. You probably don't know many of these legal concepts. How could you? That is my job. My

point is not to impress you, but to impress upon you how what you don't know can hurt you. Insurance adjusters understand these legal concepts and much more. You use an old adage, why would you bring a knife to a gunfight and deal with these trained insurance adjusters alone? What you don't know will hurt you. To make matters worse, just trying to understand the verbiage is like going to France and not speaking the French language. Why would you negotiate with someone in France when you don't even speak the language? Luckily, we do speak the language of insurance and injury claims. Think of us as your legal interpreter.

2

About The Chester Law Group Co., LPA

We are not a large impersonal law firm. We take great pride in the many long-lasting relationships we have built with our clients over the years. Our lawyers and staff understand the many physical, emotional and financial challenges and difficulties you must deal with after being seriously injured. We are dedicated to helping you recover from your injuries and obtain the quickest and largest compensation so that you can begin the process of rebuilding your life.

Here at the Chester Law Group, we are proud of the millions of dollars in settlements and verdicts we have achieved for our clients over the years. With more than 100 years of combined experience, I, along with my attorneys and co-counsel, have been successfully representing injured Ohioans just like you for a long time. Even more, we are proud of the stability and comfort we have been able to bring to our clients during their entire personal injury claim process. At the Chester Law Group, we deal with the legal and financial hassles so you can concentrate on getting better.

I cannot give legal advice in this book

The Ohio State Bar requires that I inform you that what is in this book is not legal advice. I know the arguments that insurance companies typically make, and I can make suggestions about what to look out for, but please do not take anything in this book to be legal advice. Before I can give you legal advice, I must understand the unique facts involved in your case. I cannot be your lawyer and offer specific advice unless you and I have signed an agreement that allows me to legally represent you. This book is written using Ohio law current as of the day of publication of this edition of the book. I want you to understand the landscape of personal injury and be informed about your rights. This book is a good first step in that direction.

3

Who Would Benefit From Reading This Book?

Anyone who was not at fault and has been injured in an accident can gain useful information from this book. However, this book was primarily written for those who have or may have suffered severe or catastrophic injuries or for those who have lost a loved one in an accident. When accidents cause injuries such as paralysis, traumatic brain injuries, fractures or any other injuries that leave a person permanently disabled and affect the quality of life, getting the right lawyer is extremely important. If you are severely injured or have lost a loved one in an accident, you want to make sure your rights are protected in the long term.

Why you should read this book

If you have been seriously injured in an accident, you have to take the first step in making sure that your rights are protected. Insurance companies spend a lot of money for advertising. They send out feel good messages that would have many people believe that they will be treated fairly in their personal injury claim. Wouldn't it be nice if we were "in good hands," or treated like a "good neighbor" by the insurance adjuster?

The truth is, the insurance company's goal is to pay out as little as possible for injury claims. They also do not want you to get an attorney, because they know that if you have an attorney protecting your rights, in all likelihood the more they will have to pay on your claim. In fact, one insurance company's training manual tells their adjusters to be nice to injured victims who do not have lawyers just so the person does not get a lawyer and cost the company more money. Adjusters always say that they do not pay more when an attorney is involved, but this is simply not the case.

Insurance companies routinely increase their offers when a lawyer is involved for many reasons, including the fact that the lawyer can often help the client get medical care that costs money, the lawyer helps document the case which increases its value, and the threat of lawsuits and its costs to the insurance company raise settlement offers across the board. How could they not pay out more money when an aggressive, competent lawyer increases the risk or "exposure" of a high jury verdict against the insurance company? Not taking this risk into account would be foolish on the part of the insurance company, and believe me they are not fools.

If you have been injured in an accident, you may feel overwhelmed and confused by the insurance claims-filing process. The National Association of Insurance Commissioners even recognizes the difficulty of the process and recently stressed in a consumer alert, "it is critical that claims be filed correctly to ensure you receive all the payments due to you." This book will help you to get informed about the claims process and give you tips on how to protect yourself. I commend you on taking the first step.

Don't let time run out on your claim!!!

The law imposes strict time deadlines in which to file suit for different types of actions. For example, in Ohio, a lawsuit for a motor vehicle accident typically must be filed within two years of the accident. The failure to act timely to obtain necessary medical treatment and obtain an attorney to protect you can significantly hurt your claim. While it is true that minors usually have until age 20 to file suit in most cases against the party at fault for the motor vehicle accident, they may only have two years to file a claim with their own insurance company. This is odd but true. You must talk to an experienced Ohio personal injury lawyer to determine exactly how much time you have to settle your claim or lose it forever.

It is important to know that other sorts of injuries, such as those caused by medical malpractice, may have shorter time limitations to file suit or settle the claim. For example, in general a person has one year to file a medical malpractice claim. We receive calls all the time from people who have been hurt by a doctor's negligence but lose their claim because they wait too long to contact a lawyer.

4

What Should You Receive If You Are Injured and Not at Fault?

Let's start with basic Personal Injury 101, so to speak. If you are injured due to someone else's negligence (fault), Ohio law says you are entitled to various types of damages:

• **Medical Expenses:** Reasonable and necessary medical expenses that you incur as a result of the accident or are reasonably certain to incur in the future. This includes treatment such as hospital care, diagnostic testing, surgery, physical therapy, chiropractic care and pain management. Many times the insurance companies will try to make you accept medical expenses based on what your health insurance pays. However, our attorneys may help you recover the full value of your medical expenses, not the discounted amount that the insurance company would like for you to accept. For example, if your medical bills are $10,000 but Medicaid paid the doctors $1,000 as full payment, the insurance company may argue your medical bills are only $1,000 and so only offer you $3,000 to settle. This is outrageous but true. Why should the party at fault get the benefit of you having health insurance?

• **Lost Wages:** You are also entitled to recover any wages (earnings) you lost as a result of your injuries. Wages, commissions, bonuses and all other earnings are recoverable. Even if you have used disability insurance through your employer, you can still recover the full value of your lost wages. This portion of the settlement or jury verdict is taxable.

• **Future Loss of Earnings:** If your injuries have permanently limited your ability to earn in the future, in many instances you can recover the value of your future lost income. If the medical criteria are met, our attorneys will obtain the evidence needed to support your claim and make sure you are compensated for your lost earning power over the remainder of your working years.

• **Pain and Suffering:** You should be compensated for the physical pain, mental anguish and loss of quality of life that you have suffered because of your injury. This includes future pain and suffering as well. Pain and suffering damages are in addition to, and many times exceed your medical expenses and lost wages. Many insurance companies actually use computer programs to help determine how much money to pay for pain and suffering.

• **Loss of Full Mind and Body:** Many times an accident can leave permanent injuries. If you have suffered any permanent loss of function or use of your body or mind, you should be reimbursed based on the percentage lost. This is known in the legal and medical community as a permanent impairment rating. This means you are permanently impaired as a result of the accident. Over the years, we have learned that most insurance companies only accept permanent impairment ratings from medical doctors, not chiropractors or physical therapists. As such, if you are permanently impaired, it is important that a licensed medical doctor document it.

• **Disfigurement:** If your injury has left you with scars or other unsightly marks, you should recover for that disfigurement and the embarrassment associated with it. If you never recover from the disfigurement, such as when you have a permanent scar, you may also have a permanent impairment. See above.

• **Damage to the Marital Relationship:** A marital relationship can suffer when one spouse has been severely injured. If this occurs, you are entitled to recover for the loss of care, comfort, joy, affection, assistance and loss or impairment of sexual relations. In some serious injury cases, the spouse usually has a claim against the party at fault for the "loss of consortium" they have suffered as a result of the party at fault's carelessness.

• **Death:** "Wrongful death" damages are available to the beneficiaries (often the wife, husband, parent or child) of the deceased person. Damages are not limited to economic loss and may also include lost earnings, pre-death pain and suffering and loss of consortium (loss of companionship).

• **Property Damage (damage to your vehicle):** In the case of motor vehicle accidents, if your vehicle was damaged, the insurance company of the party at fault should fix it and give you a rental car while it is getting repaired. If the damage to your vehicle is more than the value of the vehicle, the insurance company will consider it totaled and will give you money for a replacement vehicle. They will pay you the fair market value of what your vehicle was worth before the accident. This is an area where my office has seen lots of "lowball" offers over the years.

Do not make the mistake many people make - delaying or doing nothing!

You must act sooner rather than later. Doing nothing at all is one of the worst things you can do. Injuries suffered in a car accident can affect you for years to come. You want to make sure that you act before important witnesses can no longer be found, or before delays or gaps in medical treatment can damage your case. Some people may feel there is a certain stigma involved with contacting an attorney or are intimidated by the process so they don't do anything. The insurance companies hope for just this type of injured victim, the one that does not want to hire an attorney, the one that saves them money. The bottom line is that if you have been seriously injured you owe it to yourself and those you love to make sure that your rights are protected. Our attorneys and staff will make sure you feel comfortable and you will have peace of mind knowing that experienced professionals are on your side.

Over the years, we have received calls from many injured Ohioans who waited too long to see a doctor, or took actions that unknowingly destroyed their personal injury claim and denied them the justice they so rightly deserved. Don't let this happen to you. You have already been made a victim by the other person's carelessness. Don't be a victim a second time. Reading this book is a good first step. Going to my website www.chesterlaw.com and watching my on-line personal injury videos by pressing one of the three orange buttons in the middle of the home page, is another.

5

Common Insurance Company Tactics

1. Deny Liability

Liability is another way of saying who's at fault and who is supposed to pay. Before anything, the insurance company looks to see if there is any way they can deny your claim. Many clients are surprised to learn they have the burden of proof when it comes to who is at fault in the accident. It isn't enough that you were injured but you have to prove that somebody else caused the injury. Our lawyers are trained to find and present evidence regarding liability. Sometimes the insurance companies will blame you for the accident even when you are found to be innocent by police or witnesses. This is strange but true. Remember, the insurance adjuster's job is to get you to "sell" them your personal injury claim as cheap and quick as possible. For this reason, you probably should not believe everything they tell you. Remember, they usually work for the person that hurt you in the first place. If adjusters are showing up at your house or want you to come on down and settle the claim right after the accident, you should be asking yourself why? What's the rush?

2. Get the Victim to Give a Recorded Statement

The insurance adjusters are trained to get a recorded statement from the car accident victim as soon as possible. Their goal is to get you to make statements that can hurt your claim. They usually try to have you minimize your injury and need for medical care. I tell all of my clients to never talk to an adjuster without me on the phone. Anything you say will be used against you later. It is worth repeating that the adjuster usually works for the person at fault and it is their job to protect their insured and the insurance company.

3. Get the Victim to Sign a Medical Authorization Release

The insurance companies typically will send a general medical authorization for you to sign and return back to them. What they don't tell you is that you may be giving them permission to contact any medical provider you may have ever seen. There is no reason for the adjuster to see any of your medical records until a claim is actually made for your injuries. Our attorneys will make sure the insurance company only receives medical records that are relevant to your claim while insuring they do not have carte blanche access to any medical record they want. I have had several adjusters get medical records using releases signed by clients before I am involved then argue the client's injuries already existed because they had a sore neck 15 years earlier. Unbelievable!

4. Get the Victim to Agree to a Quick Settlement With a Full Release

It is very common for the insurance company to contact you very soon after the accident and offer a small amount of "inconvenience" money to settle your bodily injury claim. This may be done while you are still in pain, still seeing doctors, or before you have even had a chance to seek medical attention and find out what is wrong with you medically.

In almost every case, this quick offer is well below what is reasonable and what any competent lawyer can get a client. Accepting a sum of money for your injury, no matter how small, may destroy your chances at further recovery, even if your injuries turn out to be more serious than you thought when you accepted the settlement.

In addition, if you settle your personal injury claim without getting permission from your health insurance company, you may lose your health insurance coverage and they may not pay future medical bills. This is something most injured Ohioans don't know about. It is called "breach of subrogation" and is a legal concept that can cost you dearly if you settle your personal injury claim without a lawyer reviewing the paperwork and your case in general. Most people have never even thought to themselves, "Hey, I can lose my health insurance if I don't have a lawyer review my settlement paperwork and my case."

Some clients have actually received checks in the mail for $500 along with a release of all their rights. I guess the insurance company was hoping the client would cash the check and this would settle their claim.

Also, be wary of any auto insurance adjuster telling you that you can sign a "partial release" of your personal injury claim. Be sure to read the fine print very carefully as you may be giving up ALL of your rights.

5. Convincing the Victim that the Adjuster will Treat Them Fairly and a Lawyer will Only Cost Money

Watch out for insurance adjusters that try to befriend you and make promises to pay future medical bills. Of course they want you to think that your claim will be fairly evaluated and there is no need to contact an attorney. As mentioned above, one insurance company's training manual teaches their adjusters to keep people away from lawyers by being their friend. They do this for one reason, to save the insurance company money. The insurance companies know all too well that clients who have a competent and experienced lawyer have a greater opportunity to

gain larger settlements in general. Remember, these are trained professionals who know just what your claim is worth according to recent jury verdicts and they are trained how to negotiate a settlement that is in their favor. Don't be fooled by a nice voice on the other end of the phone who knows that you are most likely inexperienced in negotiating claims. Adjusters are by and large good people, but many of them work for companies that require them to save money by paying the least amount that you will take for your claim. It makes sense. They are in business to make money and paying you a lot of money makes them less money. The less they pay out, the more profit they make. Make sure you even the playing field!

Just because an insurance adjuster says your claim is worth X dollars does not make it true. Unless you take your case all the way to a jury, and they decide the value of your claim, your claim is ultimately worth what you will accept to settle. With a competent personal injury lawyer documenting your case and willing to go to court for you if necessary, the value of your case usually goes up. Looking at it another way, the value of your case can also be measured by the amount the insurance company will pay to reduce the risk of a larger jury verdict against them. Insurance companies hate risk. A competent, aggressive personal injury lawyer increases that risk which increases the settlement offer in most cases.

Think of lawyers and litigation like nuclear weapons. Few people want to use them, but just having them around makes you safer against the other side. When the insurance company knows you have a lawyer who has repeatedly taken them to court and made them pay properly in the past, they are more likely to pay more money to settle the claim. It only makes sense.

Talking to defense lawyers, they freely admit that they take the reputation of the lawyer into account when deciding what amount to offer. This is all part of the defense lawyer doing his job by calculating the risk to his or her client. After handling thousands of personal injury cases, it is my opinion that the more experience, competency and aggressiveness the lawyer has, the better the settlement in general, all other things being equal.

6. Disputing Medical Treatment

Many insurance companies review your claim by plugging factors from your accident into a computer program. They then determine what type of treatment is appropriate for you and how long it should take using other computer programs. Even though the adjuster is not a medical professional, he or she will usually try to deny certain medical treatments or say that you have exceeded an amount that the insurance company says is sufficient. Remember, it is only their opinion.

The fact is, medical professionals should determine what type of treatment is necessary, not the insurance companies. Almost all cases settle without going to a jury. Even so, it is a possible future jury that ultimately decides what treatment was necessary and what was not, not the insurance adjuster.

Juries don't usually believe any ridiculous arguments put forth by insurance adjusters and defense lawyers, such as waiting four days to see a doctor is a bad "gap" in treatment and the like. We protect our clients and make sure they get the medical care they are entitled to. We make sure the adjuster knows it is not them who ultimately decides the value of a case, and any evaluation must be in line with recent jury verdicts, even though very few cases ever see a jury trial.

If you don't have a lawyer, then adjusters know the case

won't be going to court or to a jury and they don't have to worry about whether their arguments make sense to a jury. They don't have to worry if a jury will buy their arguments, just whether you will buy them. If you don't buy them and decide to hire a lawyer later, it may be too late, as key witnesses, photos, or proper medical care may be unavailable or too late to get.

7. Make You Believe You Have No Case

Over the years, hearing the same adjuster arguments over and over, sometimes hundreds of times, shows us a wide variety of tactics used by adjusters. Some adjusters take the opposite tactic from being your friend. They may tell you that you have no case, that you could not have been injured in such a low speed accident, even if your injuries are serious. If you start to hear these tired arguments, be wary. Other adjusters may say that other people were not hurt in the accident so how could you be, you were only hurt because you were overweight, old, etc., juries are not awarding money, etc. Or, they may be so bold as to simply tell you they will only pay for a limited amount of treatment.

Over the years, hearing the same arguments hundreds and sometimes thousands of times, I have come to believe that these tactics are used to encourage people to settle quickly and cheaply, regardless of the cost to the injured victim. I constantly hear stories of adjusters telling clients (before they hire me) that the medical treatment was excessive without one shred of evidence to prove it. It reminds me of the old adage, just throw the spaghetti on the wall and see what sticks. If the adjuster can get you to believe your case stinks, then you will not hire a lawyer and you will settle for less than you deserve.

As you can see from the discussion above, lawyers play a big role in the injury claim process. Let's take a closer look at what an Ohio personal injury lawyer actually does.

6

What Do Lawyers Do?

For starters, lawyers protect you from the insurance company. They keep you from making statements that reduce the value of your case. They document evidence such as witness statements and any kind of damage to your body or property. They make sure the documentation is in a form that you need to give to an insurance company because it is your obligation to prove your claim.

With regard to medical providers, a lawyer will help you make sure that you receive proper diagnosis, treatment and documentation of all of your injuries. A lawyer will talk to your physician and get written reports from them to fully understand and document your medical condition. He or she will also watch to protect you from doctors who may over-bill and also help keep you out of collections.

When health insurance gets thrown in the mix, a lawyer will deal with them too. If health insurance has paid any of your medical bills they will most likely want their money back from the insurance company representing the person who hurt you. You can even jeopardize your insurance benefits if you settle a bodily injury claim without paying back your health insurance provider. Medicare and Medicaid are extremely strict when it comes to getting their money back.

Some people are surprised to find out they have to repay Medicaid, Medicare, or health insurance if they paid your personal injury related medical bills. At the Chester Law

Group, our staff will work with health insurance and in many cases reduce the amount you have to repay so there is more money left for you. Remember it is not just how much money you collect from the insurance company that matters, it is how little of that money you have to repay to medical providers and health insurers who have paid your bills up front.

7

Do You Really Need A Lawyer To Settle Your Case?

A lawyer is definitely not needed for every injury claim involving an accident. If you recovered from your injuries after minor and inexpensive treatment, and no future treatment or health problems are expected, you may do just as well in resolving your small claim on your own as if you hired a lawyer. However, it is always a good idea to run your case past an experienced personal injury lawyer just to get their opinion, as there is no such thing as too much knowledge. Most of the time, it only takes a half hour or so of your time to "pick the brain" of an experienced personal injury lawyer. By talking to a lawyer, you will most likely discover issues you never even knew existed, such as how you can lose your health insurance by settling your injury claim incorrectly. Ironically, the best way to know if you actually need to hire a lawyer is to talk to a lawyer about that very subject.

At the Chester Law Group, our lawyers primarily focus on those who have been or may be severely injured in an accident or those who have lost a loved one in an accident. However, sometimes clients come into our office and do not even know they have suffered a serious, permanent injury. I say "may be seriously injured" because many times serious injuries show up months later, and are only diagnosed after proper testing has been done. While injuries such as broken bones or cuts and bruises are obvious, many times our clients do not know the extent of their injuries when they walk in our office because they have not finished their medical care or seen a specialist who finds the serious but often times overlooked injuries, such as herniated discs, ligament injuries, and the like. Over the years, I have heard many clients tell me that they are not that hurt, only later to have their family doctor find an injury that requires surgery. In my experience, pain is not always immediately present with serious injuries.

At the Chester Law Group, we limit ourselves to those people who have or may have suffered serious injuries so that we can put all of our time and resources into helping those who need it the most. By being honest with those who may not need a lawyer to resolve their small claims, we are able to keep a manageable caseload which allows us to give you the personal attention you need and deserve.

8

10 Secrets You Should Know So You Don't Wreck Your Case

Below are some factors that can make or break your personal injury claim. There are many more, but these few give you a good idea of what you are facing when you suffer an injury in Ohio because of someone else's carelessness.

1. You are little threat to the insurance company without a lawyer

Let's be frank. Most insurance companies are profit driven machines. They evaluate each case as to the potential threat to lost money. It is a zero sum game. If you win, they lose. Unless you *are* a lawyer, if you don't have a lawyer you will not be able to file suit and be successful, so the real threat of a substantial jury verdict is very small. Since the risk to the insurance company is small, they can afford to be more aggressive with you, and they most likely will be. For example, they may have set aside, or "reserved" $200,000 for your claim, but offer you $30,000. What are you going to do about the lowball offer? After all, besides filing a complaint with the insurance commission (which will probably do very little as they don't get involved with case valuation issues) the only threat you have is that you will hire a lawyer. But, as evidence is destroyed by time or not gathered at all, that threat decreases every day, as discussed above.

Insurance adjusters love to tell injured victims that they pay the same amount regardless of whether or not a lawyer is involved or who the lawyer is, but in my experience this simply is not true.

2. Make sure you tell your doctor what hurts

The way your claim is evaluated and the dollar value it is given all depends on your medical records. It is called "documented medical evidence" in the personal injury field. Your doctor is required to detail in your records how you feel and how your injuries have affected your life, but the doctor can only put down what you tell him. Your treatment and proper recovery depends upon your relationship with your doctor, therapist and other medical care providers. Your health and recovery are always of primary importance.

The insurance company looks for key information such as the type of injuries, how long you were injured, your complaints, the doctor's findings, the type of treatment you received, and whether you will have future problems. The settlement they offer you is based on this critical medical information. If it's not in the medical records, in the insurance company's eyes, it never happened. It is this honest feedback that you give your doctor at each visit that allows the doctors to aid in your recovery. Medical records also serve under Ohio law as the foundation of your personal injury claim.

3. Gaps in treatment can harm your financial and physical recovery

The insurance companies love to look at medical records and see lots of missed appointments or inconsistent treatment. If you don't see a physician regularly, to the insurance company, it is considered evidence that you have recovered. I'm not saying you need to go to the doctor every day, but if you are in pain, it is important that you follow the instructions of your doctors and other medical providers on a regular basis to maximize your chance of recovery. Talk to your doctor about a treatment plan and stick to it. Not only do you need to make sure you are getting the treatment you need, but also if you do not regularly treat when you are in pain, your claim will suffer and you will not get the compensation you are entitled to.

4. Not following doctor's orders

Again, skipped and missed appointments really hurt your claim. If your doctor schedules you for therapy three days a week, but you only go once or twice a week, you will damage your claim. The insurance company will view these missed appointments as evidence that you must not be significantly injured because if you were, you would have made it to all of your appointments and followed the doctor's instructions. If you cannot make an appointment, make sure you tell your doctor why you missed so he can document your medical file.

5. Watch what you say

I have already mentioned how common it is for insurance companies to try to obtain a recorded statement from you. Again, I urge you to not make any statement to the insurance company without first consulting a lawyer. The insurance company will use anything you tell them against you. You have no way of knowing that the seemingly innocent question they are asking you is actually tailored to make you give an answer that can hurt your claim. Also, never lie. Even if you think it's a minor lie that does not make a difference, it can still ruin your credibility. So first, contact an experienced personal injury lawyer, and always tell the truth.

6. Keep accurate wage loss records and a diary of how you feel

It's a good idea to write down accurate accounts of your

injury and how you feel on a daily basis. This will help give important details of how your injuries have affected your every day life. Sometimes, as time goes by and your body heals, these important details can be forgotten. We tend to forget things that are uncomfortable or painful. Your diary will help you prove how severe your injuries are which can strengthen your claim. It is also important that you keep track of any time you missed from work, including time off for doctor appointments. You will want to make sure your doctor is documenting your missed work as well as writing excuses for your absences.

7. Make sure you tell your attorney about any past accidents or injuries

Your lawyer is on your side and it goes without saying that you must be open and honest regarding any past accidents or injuries you may have had. There is no benefit to withholding this information from your attorney. Some clients fear that if their prior history is revealed a lawyer will not take their case. The reality is, the insurance companies almost always uncover prior incidents and medical treatment, and the failure to reveal them hurts your claim much more than the actual prior injury does. Your attorney can help you determine if your prior injuries are legally significant or not, but he/she cannot help you if it is kept a secret. Insurance companies have access to claims databases that can show all past medical treatments paid by insurance. Better to be up front and honest from the beginning than have your credibility questioned which may be even more damaging.

8. Not being honest about your activity level

You must also be honest with your lawyer and your medical providers about what you can and cannot do. Make sure you tell your doctor if you can no longer walk, bend, climb or participate in hobbies like you used to before your accident. Whether you can live your life with the level of activity you had prior to your accident is an important part of your claim. However, if you do not reveal your true level of function, your doctor cannot treat you properly and in

addition your credibility can be destroyed. In many serious accident cases, insurance companies hire private investigators to conduct surveillance of you and your residence. If you claim that you cannot run, climb or bend over and then are caught on videotape doing these things, it can be very damaging to your claim.

9. Be sure to get permission from your health insurance company to settle your personal injury claim

In many cases your own health insurance company pays your accident related bills and then gets repaid at settlement time by the careless person's insurance company. This usually keeps your bills out of collections. You may have a contract with your health insurance company to repay them for accident related medical bills they paid and not even know it. Your health insurance company usually has the right to get their money back from the party at fault's insurance company for medical bills they paid from your accident. This is called "the right of subrogation." For example, in the case of a motor vehicle accident, "AAA health insurance company" may pay your medical bills from the car accident, and they have a right to get their money back from the careless guy's auto insurance company when the case settles. If you don't have their permission, you may breach your contract with them and may lose your health insurance. Also, if you will be having future care, you need to let them know about this to get their informed consent to pay the future bills after the personal injury case is settled. Failure to do this may mean they will not pay the future bills. If you do not repay your health insurance, they may sue you to get their money. Medicare and the Bureau of Workers' Compensation may require you to place part of your settlement aside for future treatment before they pay future accident related bills. In the case of Medicare, if you don't you could lose your coverage.

10. You may not have to repay your health insurance company for bills they have paid for injuries caused by the accident

Many clients are surprised that they do not always have to repay their private health insurance companies, or government health insurance, like Bureau of Workers' Compensation,

Medicaid, or Medicare, for medical bills they paid from the accident, and they can keep their benefits also. There are many situations where you do not have to repay them some or all of the money they spent on your accident related medical care. Don't just pay them back blindly. An experienced personal injury attorney can reduce or eliminate repayment in many situations. Remember, it is not just the amount of money that you get from the insurance company that matters, it is how much of it you get to keep and legally not repay to health insurance while keeping your health benefits. This is especially true in catastrophic injury cases where many times we can eliminate repayment of health insurance payments made. The savings may be more than the legal fee, and can easily justify hiring an experienced personal injury lawyer in serious injury cases, even when the insurance company has already offered their entire insurance policy limits to you. I bet you did not know that.

9

The Number One Mistake Injured Ohioans Make In Their Injury Claims

This may come as no surprise, but the number one mistake injured Ohioans make when trying to handle their own personal injury case is they fail to realize all of the pitfalls in the process and they trust the insurance adjuster without seeking independent advice from a lawyer, whether or not they actually end up hiring a lawyer. Luckily for you, you have begun to avoid this largest of all pitfalls by reading this book. Sometimes knowing that you are "in over your head" and taking steps to remedy this lack of information is the smartest and bravest move a person can make. What you don't know will harm you. Just as you would hire a brain surgeon to do brain surgery, it is wise to hire an experienced injury lawyer to handle this complex area of law.

10

Some Tips On Hiring An Ohio Injury Lawyer

In this day and age, auto insurance companies are fighting almost all claims vigorously and litigating a significant number of lawsuits. This is why it is important to hire a personal injury lawyer whom you trust is capable and willing to go to court for you, all the way to jury for you, if necessary. While of course no one factor is determinative of a good outcome to your claim, in my experience, without the threat of a lawsuit, the auto insurance companies don't have any real risk, such as a negative jury verdict.

There are many Ohio personal injury lawyers and law firms who litigate their clients' claims all the way to a jury when needed. It is important to hire an experienced personal injury attorney who will go to court and fight for your rights.

Another issue you will want to discuss with your lawyer is whether or not he will put up his or her own money to finance litigation and not require you to pay him or her back if you lose. If a lawyer does not advance costs of litigation, he or she may not believe in your case, or may not have the financial resources to pay for experts that are necessary to get top dollar. You don't want a personal injury lawyer who tries to save money and does things on a shoestring budget at the cost of a good settlement or verdict.

I would also go to the lawyer's website and read or watch client testimonials. What former clients think of a lawyer and his or her staff can tell you a lot about how you will be treated. While no two cases are alike, if the lawyer has raving fans as former clients, you can probably assume the lawyer did a good job for them and they were happy with the legal services and personal service they received.

Personally, I suggest that your lawyer's litigation history and actual client results be your starting point. Once again, filing suit to get a fair settlement is needed more and more these days, and in these days of lower and lower settlement offers in Ohio, an experienced lawyer who is willing to repeatedly fight for his clients in court is essential to a good result. If any personal injury lawyer you talk to says he settles almost all of his cases outside of court, it has to make you wonder how you can get a good result in the current, low offer climate in Ohio.

While every case is different, as a general rule if your Ohio car accident attorney won't answer the above questions to your satisfaction, I suggest you continue your lawyer search. Results are what matter. The days of quick fair settlements outside of court without an experienced, seasoned lawyer are ending, so pick your lawyer wisely.

Another factor to consider when hiring an Ohio personal injury lawyer is how the lawyers and staff at the lawyer's office treat you and how you feel when interacting with them. I think it is a good idea to trust your gut when hiring a lawyer.

- Are you comfortable with the lawyer and their staff in your initial contact?

- Are all of your questions answered fully and respectfully

in your initial meeting?

- Are you meeting with an actual personal injury lawyer, just a paralegal or no one at all?

- Does it seem that they care about you and your needs?

- Do you get a gut feeling that the lawyer and staff will "go to bat" for you or does it just seem like they are going through the motions and you are just another number?

- Do you feel the lawyer values you and your claim?

- Does your lawyer and his or her staff return your phone calls promptly?

- Are you the lawyer's number one concern?

These questions are important because you will most likely be entering into an important, long-term relationship with the lawyer and his or her staff. It is important that your gut reaction be that you trust them to take care of you or someone you love. With your experienced lawyer's help and guidance, you will be making important decisions that can affect the rest of your life. It is important that your lawyer be a partner in this process with you. I also suggest you consider hiring a lawyer who spends most or all of his time doing personal injury law. Many lawyers handle personal injury claims, but fewer have both the knowledge and the experience to effectively deal with all of the complicated, changing laws in the Ohio personal injury field. To put it another way, you probably would not hire a general surgeon to do delicate brain surgery on you, would you?

11

Why You Should
Hire Us

From our years of experience, we at the Chester Law Group believe that injured Ohioans who are well informed about the injury claim process make the best clients. They also usually end up happier at the end of the process, all things being equal. This book is just the first step. We will earn your trust by keeping you updated and informed every step of the way. While we are known for aggressively pursuing our clients' rights in court and with juries, as evidenced by some recent settlements shown below, I believe that our personal attention is one of the main reasons we receive numerous referrals from our growing family of clients as well as from other lawyers and professionals.

We will listen to all of your concerns, answer all of your questions, and work to make sure that the person responsible for your injury fully compensates you for your losses. We are committed to protecting your rights while handling your case with professionalism, compassion and aggressive advocacy. We have the dedication and experience to help you successfully make it through your serious personal injury claim.

Thank you for taking the time to read this book. I hope you found it useful and we look forward to helping you with your personal injury claim.

I believe that if you have read this far, you or someone you love has some real problems to deal with.

1. You don't trust the insurance company that is

probably calling you hounding you for a recorded statement or to sign papers.

2. You may not know how to get desperately needed, quality medical care for your accident related injuries, and...

3. You don't know which lawyer to choose to get the insurance company off of your back and eventually force the insurance company to offer you a fair settlement.

I can help you solve all of those problems and more. I have done it for many other injured Ohioans, as the client comments listed in the following chapter show, and I can help do it for you. Don't believe me – believe what my clients say. Call me now at 1-800-218-4243 and start a relationship with me and with all of us at Chester Law Group that will see you through this difficult situation. I believe that you will be glad you made the call. Please call now before you say or do something that seriously damages your injury claim. Get the help you need from lawyers you can trust.

Appendix A: Client Comments

What my clients say about Chester Law Group

Kathryn and Keith Zumsteg

When I had problems with my surgery after being hit by a SUV, Chester Law Group was right there for us. We were stopped at a red light when a SUV plowed straight into us from behind. We were in quite a bit of pain and did not know how to proceed with this. As far as Chester Law Group, I do not know where we would be without them and their assistance. They have genuine and sincerity I feel. I think I am pretty good at recognizing that. The paralegals are a keeper. One hundred percent customer service. Genuine. They always asked how we were doing. Seemed like there was never a delay. You can tell the lawyers at Chester Law Group have a genuine side to them. Not just the legal stuff. They have that compassionate side I don't think you would expect to find in an attorney.

Thank You Chester Law Group.

Keith Zumsteg from Columbus Ohio. Keith suffered through several lumbar surgeries caused by an SUV accident.

Kathryn Zumsteg

Whenever I had a question my paralegal was always there to answer my question. The lawyers are wonderful. They came to meet with us a couple of days after my husband got out of the hospital. There was no way that we could have made the trip.

He came all the way to our house. He has that special touch. I don't have any concerns or fears. I feel that they have been there and are there whenever we have needed them.

Kathryn Zumsteg from Columbus, Ohio. Kathryn suffered with herniated disc injuries from an SUV accident.

I would have made a very bad decision if it wasn't for Attorney David Chester. I was ready to settle for less than a 3rd of what I got. Thanks to David Chester. Eugene D.

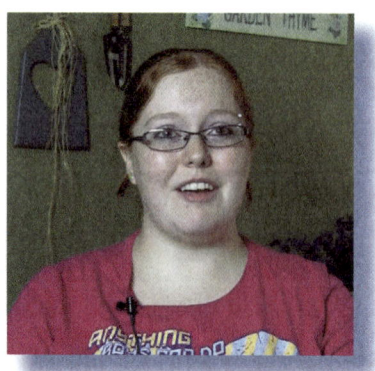

Laura Weaver

The settlement I got with Chester law Group was amazing. I did not really expect it to be like that. It was great. It helped out a lot. Vince (from Chester Law Group) was very kind. I really enjoyed working with him. He explained everything clearly. They treated me very well ... all the staff. I am very grateful. You helped out a lot. I think they are the best choice.

Laura Weaver from Orwell, Ohio. Laura suffered a brain injury and other serious bodily injuries in an Ohio car accident.

Attorney Chester is someone who cares and wants to protect the injured. Susan B.

I strongly feel that without Attorney David Chester, I would not have been fully informed of my legal rights regarding the auto accident and I would not have received the proper care.
Dina N.

Attorney Chester provides a very valuable service. Alvin S.

Zach Rayburn

Chester Law actually went the extra mile. My wife decided to leave and they helped me out, no charge really. Everything has been quite satisfactory, I think.

Tom has been great, especially helpful. I could give him a call whenever I had a question. I especially liked that David came down and talked to me personally at my home. I had to make very few trips up to the office, they came to see me. Vince is a really nice guy.

The whole process is really rough but these guys make it a whole lot easier. Without them I would have nothing but actually I am going to have something that is quite reasonable considering what was available.

A guy pulled out in front of me while I was riding my motorcycle and nearly killed me. I was in the hospital for 5 months which left me paralyzed from the chest down.

I picked Chester Law because David had a similar experience and when he talked to me I believed he would fight for me and I believe he has.

I think they are honest guys and if I would need a lawyer I would come back.

Zach Rayburn from Wooster, Ohio. Motorcycle accident paraplegic.

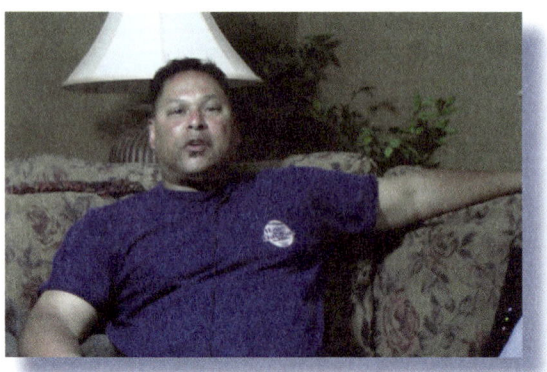

Benjamin Coleman

I have been to the big law groups that you see on TV but I would have never gotten the personal detail that I received from the Chester Law Group. The Chester Law Group staff and especially Tom Haskins treated me like a person and not a number.

They gave me step-by-step what was going to happen in litigation. In mediation Tom told me what to expect and I felt very comfortable leaving it up to him.

I could not have ask for a better attorney than Tom Haskins. When the settlement closed not only did I find a new attorney that I would recommend to anyone but I have also developed a new friendship.

I felt that Tom was not handling my case for the monetary gain but that he wanted to right the wrong and bring justice to me.

I was very satisfied with my settlement.

Benjamin Coleman, Jackson Township, Ohio. Benjamin suffered wrist injuries from a motorcycle accident.

Keith Day

My whole experience with Chester Law Group was phenomenal. I think if you are ever hurt or injured and need legal representation I can recommend them with an open and full heart. They are fantastic people and will meet your needs. I would go with Chester Law Group over anyone else. I was going down the turnpike west and was in construction and a truck changed lanes and pushed me into the concrete barrier. He took off. I hit my head. My vehicle was totaled. I had a herniated disc. I had three months of physical therapy and 2 epidurals. I have never sued anybody. I have helped so many people over my career but the only people who helped me was Chester Law Group. Kathy was awesome and friendly. Almost like I was not talking to an attorney or paralegal, but rather a good friend trying to see me through a tough time.

Keith Day

Firefighter from Berea, Ohio

Kyle Csortos

I was driving to work and a truck in the incoming lane crashed into my car causing my car to flip many times. It gave me a back injury and a head injury. The next day an insurance adjuster came to my house and I did not know what to do. I had heard of Chester Law Group. Jackie was an amazing paralegal. She helped me with everything. Any question I asked she answered. Vince Kloss is a great attorney. He was always there to answer any questions I had. Anyone with injuries like mine or their own injuries should consider having Chester Law Group as their attorney.

Kyle Csortos

Millbury, OH

I am very grateful Attorney Chester and his staff made my life easier. I'm not afraid to call them and get answers to all the questions that I've had, and no worries. Thank You.

Sally S.

Susanne Morely

My name is Susanne Morely and I live in Painesville, Ohio. Chester Law Group is there, they know exactly what they are doing, they know how to talk to people, they answered every question I had. I love Chester Law Group. I definetly recommend Chester Law Group for anyone who has been in an accident.

I was at a red light and a car coming from south to north ran her red light and hit me. My injuries are a torn rotator cuff, I have 4 herniated discs in my neck, and horrible headaches from the accident.

I have had surgery on the rotator cuff, physical therapy, and injections in the back of my neck for the headaches. Going through the injuries was the bad part but having Chester Law Group there to talk to, it was awesome, I could not have asked for better. Anybody in which I had talked to at Chester Law Group was awesome especially Vince and Jackie. Jackie, I just love her. She is just like my sister. I can call her she calls me back, she explained everything I needed to do in detail step by step. You could not ask for a better person.

I had to call Vince a couple of times and he called me back within the hour. He called right back and answered every question I had. The settlement I received was very fair. The Chester Law Group is the one I would call again.

Susanne Morely from Painesville, Ohio suffers with torn rotator cuff and herniated discs in her neck from a car accident.

I very much appreciate the help from my attorney's quick response. Thank you very much. Michael R.

I am glad that I called Attorney Chester. James W.

Attorney Chester provides very valuable information that I'm going to benefit from in the long run. Michele B.

Thank God for David Chester. He helped me get the medical attention I needed and the compensation I deserved. Christine S.

Attorney Chester enabled me to make all the correct decisions and obtain the required information, medical care and documents that I would not have been able to do on my own. I was very confident and satisfied with Mr. Chester and his staff. Kathleen B.

I was glad that Attorney Chester was willing to help me. Donna L.

I was told I would be in a wheelchair by a doctor. Thanks to Attorney Chester and the expert medical care he helped me get, I am walking good. Delcie L.

Jamie Madigan

I found Chester Law Group on the internet. I thought maybe I should get a lawyer for this as it would be more than I could handle. They came out to my house the very next day. With the Chester Law Group you can feel real confident and comfortable that they are going to explain everything and guide you through the steps and make it easier than what it could be.

About my accident: I was on the way home from work on a Friday afternoon and I noticed a car that was broke down half way in a driveway. I figured I would stop and push her into the driveway and get her out of the road. As I started pushing the car a girl slammed right into the car I was pushing at about 45 MPH which sent me flying through the air.

I broke my fibula, blew both my knees out and had some other injuries. It was pretty scary. I had a couple of surgeries, I had both my knees done and I was out of work for 8 months.

This is the first time I have had anything like this happen. There was a lot going on and I was worried about my rights, who would be paying for all of this, and I missed so much work. I actually got to work with Jackie at Chester Law, she was great ever since day one. She explained everything to me. She explained the whole process, what was going to happen, and what I could expect. In fact she even sent me flowers after one of my surgeries which was great as it really brightened my day.

Vince came out two days after I contacted Chester Law. He was great, came right out to the house. I really nice guy, and explained everything in layman's terms. He made it real understandable. There is a lot going on when something like this happens. You get kind of nervous and worried so you need someone to explain what is going to happen and what to expect and Vince was really good about that.

I would definitely recommend Chester Law just for the security that you know that they are on your side and they are going to answer questions for you and help because this is going to be a long road ahead of you when anything like this happens. Jamie Madigan, Medina Ohio

I was pleased with the timely legal help you provided when I had my automobile accident. Asenith C.

Attorney Chester protected me from the auto insurance companies. Lena V.

The accident turned our whole lives upside down. I thank our attorney for all his help in this. Frances B.

Attorney Chester helped me get fair treatment regarding my accident. Judy S.

I did not realize there was any help out there for me. I thank you for your help and support. Fran H.

Cassandra Hill

The Chester Law Group staff- they are amazing. They went out of there way, they came to where we were. Every call I made to the office was answered in a timely manner and they would always get someone on the line. The first accident I was hit from behind waiting to turn into my driveway. I had bruising, neck injuries, and I had to go through physical therapy.

In a 2nd accident we were pedestrians standing watching a live nativity when this girl pulled into the side of a truck and the truck lost control and came up over the curb and plowed into 4 of us that were standing there as a group. The next thing I knew I was flying through the air, my brother was hit and a friend Eli was injuried seriously, it was pretty bad.

My brother died that night of the accident at Metro going into surgery. They took me down to CAT Scan and at that time they told me they did not find anything, but since then I am going into surgery for problems with my neck.

The first case is settled but with the 2nd one there was a lawsuit. The Chester Law Group is wonderful, use them, do not try to handle a case like this by yourself.

Cassandra Hill from Ashtabula, Ohio, suffers with serious neck injuries from a pedestrian accident.

Dwight Williams

We were standing watching a Christmas nativity at the church and I heard a bang and saw a car coming towards me... the next thing I knew I went flying through the air and I ended up laying on the ground.

I ended up with wrist and knee injuries, a #4 in my back and a fractured knee and I have been fighting these injuries ever since.

I would recommend them, highly recommend them as attorneys. I talked to Jackie, Shawna, and David Chester and everyone I talk to has been really, really nice and I have had no problems. And I would highly recommend them as an attorney because I do not think he would every give up on it.

Dwight Williams of Ashtabula Ohio

I don't know what I would have done without them. Robert N.

If it were not for Attorney Chester, I would have had to pay several thousands of dollars out of my pocket for doctor expenses. James H.

Jeff Baker

I would definitely recommend Chester Law to help you through all the finances and after dealing with the insurance company first, never do it.

The people I talked to on the phone were great, I loved them. That is why I wanted to come see them.

Easy to work with, the personalities were great. I just liked it.

Everything went smooth. I just ran out of patience a couple of times but they talked me through it, I was happy from there on.

Jeff Baker from Minerva, Ohio suffers from a knee injury.

The information Attorney Chester provided and the timely manner in which I received it truly made a difference. Kristy L.

I was very pleased with my attorney and the help he gave me. Michael P.

Attorney Chester gave me peace of mind. Tamera S.

Thank God I had the help from David Chester. Kathy M.

Attorney Chester guided me through the corrupt system. Mark M.

Because of Attorney Chester I was able to get through everything and get my neck and upper back treated. Mr. Chester and his staff were honest and worked in my best interests. I am thankful. Jeffrey W.

The information Attorney Chester provided helped me not answer questions from adjusters, claims representatives, etc. Keep up the good work. Linda D.

Let me say our family is extremely grateful to your law firm for the prompt, efficient and effective service we have received. Michael C.

I would like to thank Attorney Chester. Without him I would have held off care for fear of the medical expenses. After talking with him, I was able to get the care that I needed. I only wish I'd talked to him sooner. Aaron H.

Attorney Chester assists those of us in need, in shock, at the very time that we need representation the most. Barbara B.

Without the services of Attorney Chester, I would not have known where to go to get help. I would have been injured and not known the extent of my injury, where to go for medical treatment, or know who to talk to about compensation for my pain and suffering. Maggie G.

DISCLAIMER: The above client comments and references to any case results are specific to the facts and legal circumstances of each of the below clients' cases and should not be used to form an expectation that the same financial results could be obtained for other clients in similar matters without reference to the specific factual and legal circumstances of each clients case.

Appendix B: Our Cases, Verdicts and Results

Our cases, verdicts and results

At the Ohio offices of Chester Law Group Co. LPA, our case results speak for themselves. See the settlement and verdict amounts below for a wide range of cases. I have listed a few confidential settlements first so as to not hint at their value. Cases are not in perfect value order.

DISCLAIMER: The results are specific to the facts and legal circumstances of each of the clients' cases and should not be used to form an expectation that the same results could be obtained for other clients in similar matters without reference to the specific factual and legal circumstances of each client's case. Litigation co-counsel is listed where appropriate.

Confidential Settlement – Motor Vehicle Accident: Quadriplegic Spinal Cord Injury with Economic damages over $12,000,000.00. Chester Law Group counseled attorney Nick Degennaro in handling the case of a middle aged man from central Ohio who was catastrophically injured when he was hit by a car owned by an employee of a major telecommunications company. The client suffered a severe spinal cord injury leaving him a permanent quadriplegic. Medical bills, lost wages and other economic damages are expected to be over $12,000,000.00. Confidential Settlement: January 2021.

Confidential Settlement – Motor Vehicle Accident: Paraplegic Spinal Cord Injury with Economic damages over

$5,000,000.00. Our client, a young male from Northeast Ohio, was catastrophically injured while riding his motorcycle when the driver of a car pulled out from a stop sign. This caused our client to hit the car and propelled our client off of his bike. Our client suffered a severe spinal cord injury leaving him a permanent paraplegic. Medical bills, lost wages and other economic damages are expected to be over $5,000,000.00. The settlement amount is confidential. We ended up also fighting with Medicaid to reduce the amount we have to repay them for accident-related bills they paid because of recent U.S. Supreme Court case law that made Ohio's Medicaid subrogation statute unconstitutional. That fight has lasted into 2018. Litigation co-counsel was Tom Haskins.

Confidential Settlement – Wrongful Death: Truck Accident. Our client, a young man from northeast Ohio, was killed by a truck owned by a national commercial trucking company that turned in front of him. Settlement: confidential in September 2019.

Confidential Settlement – Industrial Accident: Paraplegic Spinal Cord Injury with $4,000,000.00 in Economic Damages. Our client suffered a catastrophic spinal cord injury in an industrial accident. The injury resulted in our client becoming a paraplegic. Medical bills and lost wages are expected to be more than $4,000,000.00. Liability was in serious doubt. Further details are prohibited by the terms of the nondisclosure agreement. Litigation co-counsel was Lynn

Lazarro. Settlement: confidential in January 2014.

Confidential Settlement – Wrongful Death: Railroad Accident: 12-Year-Old Boy Killed. Our client was a 12-year-old Northwest Ohio boy who was out walking near parked train cars in his backyard. The railroad company moved the trains and ran over the little boy. We argued that the railroad company was negligent for not inspecting the train tracks before moving train cars and for violating their own safety protocols. After extensive litigation discovery, we negotiated a confidential settlement in November of 2013. Liability was very weak. Confidentiality and secrecy are often conditions of settlement in these types of cases. Litigation co-counsel was Larry Scanlon. Settlement: confidential in November 2013.

Jury Verdict / Confidential Settlement: $3,100,000.00 – Our client, a middle-aged Northeast Ohio woman, went in for routine surgery. She checked the box stating she was allergic to a medication used in anesthesia. She identified the drug she was allergic to. The anesthesiologist gave her that drug and she ended up with serious injuries, including brain damage leading to memory loss. Litigation co-counsel was Chris Mellino. The hospital made a confidential settlement before the jury trial. Attorney Mellino went to trial against the doctors involved and received a $3,100,000.00 jury verdict in September 2013. Case remanded for a new trial. Case settled before second trial. Settlement: confidential in January 2020.

$1,700,000.00 Default Judgment – Motorcycle

Collision: Our client, a 27-year-old female from Jefferson County was involved in motorcycle accident as a passenger. The driver was speeding and lost control. Our client suffered a serious closed head injury and multiple facial and body fractures. Suit was filed with co-counsel Nick Degennaro and a default judgment was obtained in favor of our client for $1,700,000.00 (defendant did not defend case). Collection efforts have been unsuccessful. July 2015.

$1,275,000.00 – Our client suffered a traumatic brain injury affecting eyes, and was forced to retire as truck driver. Litigation co-counsel was Lori Luka.

$1,100,000.00 – Traumatic Injury to Mother and Unborn Child/Cuyahoga County/Premises Liability/ Wrongful Death. Our pregnant client was severely injured by a motor vehicle while sitting on a bench in front of a commercial establishment. Injuries resulted in a child born with severe brain damage and multiple disabilities. Sadly, the child died within a year of the accident. Liability attached to the premises owner for unsafe condition of the customer parking in relation to the bench. Our investigation uncovered a prior incident and notice to the premises owner of the unsafe condition. Primary recovery from the premises owner for Injuries and Wrongful Death with litigation co-counsel Lori Luka. Total awarded for injuries and Wrongful Death: $1,100,000.00

$1,000,000.00 Settlement – Our client, an Ohio woman was pregnant and went to her local hospital complaining of severe abdominal pain. The hospital knew that she was pregnant but failed to use baby monitor or do an ultrasound. The mother had internal bleeding which resulted in the death of her unborn child. A lawsuit was filed and a settlement reached quickly after. Our sincerest sympathies go out to her and her family. Litigation co-counsel was Chris Mellino This tragedy could have been avoided if the hospital staff had followed established legal guidelines for the treatment of pregnant women with abdominal pain. March 2015.

$850,000.00 Settlement – Our client, an Ohio resident in her eighties, went in for treatment of kidney stones. It was our position that the doctor did not do the proper testing to determine if the kidney stones were toxic. When the doctor dissolved the kidney stones, the toxic remains killed our client. We co-counseled this claim with Chris Mellino which settled for $850,000.00 before trial. There was very little in economic damages due to our client's advanced age. We are sorry for her family's loss. Settlement: $850,000.00 in January 2013.

$850,000.00 Settlement – Our client, a 63 year old man from Medina, suffered back and neck injuries in a car accident that required surgery. We settled the case April, 2021 before trial with co-counsel Lori Luka.

$800,000.00 Settlement / Motor Vehicle Accident: Torn Arm Muscles and Injured Knee. Our client was a middle aged Ohio man who was injured in a motor vehicle accident while on the job. He suffered torn muscles in both arms and an injury to his knee that will likely require future surgery. He continues to have pain in his arms and pain in his knee as of February 2015.

$752,500.00 – Child from Cleveland suffered brain injured that resulted in death. Lori Luka was litigation co-counsel.

$750,000.00 – Our client was an elderly woman from western Ohio who suffered back injuries after being hit by a drunk driver. She needed several back surgeries. Pre-existing active conditions were an issue. Litigation co-counsel was Nick Degennaro.

$650,000.00 Settlement – Car Accident: Elderly Michigan Resident Killed in One-Car Accident. Our client, an elderly Michigan man, was killed when his friend lost control of the vehicle the friend was driving in Ohio. Our client left behind a loving wife and daughter. Economic damages, such as lost wages, were over $1,000,000.00. The insurance company for the party at fault fought liability and injury causation during litigation but a settlement was reached in January 2014 just before trial. Litigation co-counsel was Tom Haskins. Settlement: $650,000.00 in January 2014.

Insurance Policy Limits – Motorcycle Accident: Knee Injury in Northern Ohio. A middle-aged Northern Ohio male was involved in a motorcycle accident. He suffered several injuries that required several surgeries and rehabilitation. Settlement: policy limits.

Insurance Policy Limits – Wrongful Death Trailer Crash: Husband/Father Killed. Our client, an Ohio resident, husband and father, was a passenger in a vehicle pulling an enclosed trailer. The driver of the vehicle failed to negotiate a left hand turn and our client was ejected from the vehicle and subsequently died. We are sorry for his family's loss. Very limited auto insurance. Settlement: insurance policy limits.

Insurance Policy Limits – Truck Accident: Lacerated Hand With Multiple Surgeries and Pulmonary Embolism. Our client, a 42-year-old man from Akron, Ohio, was involved in a four-car collision which included a truck. Our client suffered several lacerated tendons in his left hand and his postoperative course was complicated by a pulmonary embolism. The party who caused the motor vehicle collision was liable for the pulmonary embolism as well as the surgery charges since the embolism happened post-surgery and the surgery was necessitated by the collision. Our client underwent a second surgery, extensor tenolysis to his left hand and capsulotomy of his wrist. Litigation co-counsel was Lynn Lazarro. Medical bills totaled more than $77,000.00. Insurance was insufficient. Settlement: insurance policy limits.

Insurance Policy Limits – Truck Accident: Compression Fractures, Summit County. A 55-year-old man living in Youngstown was involved in a three-vehicle accident on SR 8 in Akron. He sustained compression fractures after a car tried to change lanes and ran into the front of his truck. Joe

Joseph was litigation co-counsel. Insurance was insufficient. Settlement: insurance policy limits.

Insurance Policy Limits – Motorcycle Accident: Burst Fracture of Spine. Our young client was riding on his motorcycle when he suffered a catastrophic back injury at the hands of a careless driver. He suffered a burst fracture of his spine and required extensive surgery to repair his back. He was in therapy for an extended period of time and will have pain and suffering and potential future medical treatment for the rest of his life. Auto insurance was insufficient. Settlement: insurance policy limits.

Insurance Policy Limits – Wrongful Death Auto Collision: 82-Year-Old Woman. Our client, an 82-year-old woman from Columbus, Ohio, was killed in an auto collision in Franklin County, Ohio. The party at fault went left of center and struck the vehicle my client was in. Sadly, my client suffered for a period of time after the collision and subsequently died as a result of her injuries. We are sorry for her family's loss. Settlement: insurance policy limits.

$526,000 Settlement – Our client, a 25 year old female from western Ohio, broke both her arms which required surgery when an escaped cow crossed the road in front of her. The case settled June, 2021 before trial with co-counsel Lori Luka.

$525,000.00 – A 45-year-old man from Grand Rapids, Ohio, was involved in a collision with a semi. He suffered several broken bones, lacerations, a concussion and lost 3 teeth.

$500,000 – A northern Ohio male seriously injured his knee as well as other, less serious bodily injuries when he was hit by a motor vehicle. He required extensive knee surgery as well as rehabilitation of the knee.

$500,000.00 – Our client, who lived alone, died from Covid which was brought to her by a hospital employee treating her for a car accident.

$500,000.00 – **Jury Verdict:** Akron man was injured in a bar fight and suffered brain injuries that required rehabilitation and a hospital stay. Jury verdict against men who beat him up. Lynn Lazarro was litigation co-counsel.

$362,500.00 – **Trucking Accident: Fractured Wrist, Multiple Disk Herniations.** Our client, a 58-year-old man living in Tippecanoe, Ohio was involved in a trucking accident when a semi tractor-trailer failed to maintain an assured clear distance and struck his vehicle in the rear. The client suffered a fractured wrist and multiple disk herniations requiring surgery. Settlement: $362,500.00 in April 2015.

$300,000.00 (policy limits) – Amount awarded to two 18 year old Eastern Ohio residents involved in an automobile accident causing severe injuries, including a life flight.

$300,000.00 – A middle-aged man suffered a closed head injury after a head-on collision in Summit County.

$295,000.00 – Alliance man injured in auto accident. Client suffered cervical disc injuries requiring surgery.

$282,000.00 – Lorain man injured in motor vehicle collision. Client suffered multiple herniated discs requiring several back surgeries.

$260,000.00 Jury Verdict – Insurer Refused to Pay Limit in Cuyahoga County. Cuyahoga County jury verdict for driver injured in a collision where insurer refused to pay policy limits of $100,000.00 to settle the claim. Jury verdict of $260,000.00 forced insurer to pay in excess of policy limits. Litigation co-counsel was Joe Joseph of Cleveland Ohio. Jury verdict: $260,000.00.

$250,000.00 Settlement – Car Accident: Man Hit from Behind Causing Surgical Neck Injury. Our client was a 43-year-old man from Cleveland, Ohio, who was involved in an accident in Newton, Ohio. Our client was driving on the Ohio turnpike when he slowed down to avoid a tarp in the road. He was then hit from behind by another car and suffered several injuries including a neck injury which required surgery to repair. The client made a full recovery. A lawsuit was filed and a settlement reached before trial. Litigation co-counsel was Lynn Lazarro. Settlement: $250,000.00 in October 2014.

$250,000.00 – A 77-year-old woman from Parma, Ohio was T-boned by a car. She suffered a fractured right knee and wrist.

$247,500.00 – A Canton woman was involved in a serious auto accident. Client suffered heel and ankle injuries requiring multiple surgeries.

$165,000.00 – A 55-year-old Akron schoolteacher was

thrown from his motorcycle when a tow-truck pulled into his lane of travel. Client sustained multiple fractures and ACL tear that required surgery.

$154,500.00 – Car Accident: Wrongful Death of Middle-aged Northeast Ohio Man. Our client was a middle-aged man from Northeast Ohio. He was killed in an auto accident. His future lost wages and other economic damages totaled almost $900,000.00. Liability was in doubt on this case. We argued that the party at fault crossed a double yellow line on the road. The case was settled before a jury trial was necessary. Our sincere condolences to his family. Litigation co-counsel was Nick Degennaro. Settlement: in January 2014.

$145,000.00 – A 42-year-old female suffered multiple injuries when she was rear-ended in Brecksville.

$125,000.00 (policy limits) – A 22-year-old North Royalton man was injured while a passenger in a friend's car. Injuries to his hip and wrist required surgery and rehabilitation.

$105,050.00 – A 64-year-old Cuyahoga County man received non-surgical neck, shoulder and back injuries when he was rear-ended and subsequently pushed into a third vehicle.

$100,000.00 (policy limits) – A 45-year-old Summit County man suffered multiple disc herniations due to auto accident requiring surgery.

$100,000.00 (policy limits) – A 33-year-old Lake County man suffered a non-surgical lumbar herniated disc after being rear ended by a truck.

We Are Here For You *20 Offices Throughout Ohio*

Akron ....
430 White Pond Drive
Akron, OH 44320 Phone: 330-253-5678

Amherst ....
199 N. Leavitt Rd. Suite 201
Amherst, OH 44001

Canton ....
4884 Higbee Ave. NW Suite 200
Canton, OH 44718

Cleveland East Beachwood ....
3401 Enterprise Pkwy. Suite 340-691
Beachwood, OH 44122

Cleveland North ....
850 Euclid Ave. Suite 1003
Cleveland, OH 44114

Cleveland South Independence ....
5005 Rockside Rd. Suite 600-691
Independence, OH 44131

Cleveland West Westlake ....
1991 Crocker Rd. Suite 600-691
Westlake, OH 44145

Columbus North ....
1900 Polaris Pkwy. Suite 450-691
Columbus, OH 43240

Columbus Downtown ....
35 E. Gay St. Suite 510
Columbus, OH 43215

Cincinnati ....
8044 Montgomery Rd. Suite 700
Cincinnati, OH 45236

Dayton ....
70 Birch Alley Suite 240, Building B
Beavercreek, OH 45440

Medina ....
3637 Medina Rd. Suite 350
Medina, OH 44256

Mentor ....
7408 Center St.
Mentor, OH 44060

Ravenna ....
231 S. Chestnut St.
Ravenna, OH 44266

Toledo South Maumee ....
1715 Indian Wood Cir. 2nd Floor
Maumee, OH 43537

Toledo Downtown ....
420 Madison Ave Suite 520
Toledo, OH 43604

Twinsburg ....
2112 Case Pkwy S. Suite 9
Twinsburg, OH 44087

Warren ....
526 Niles Cortland Rd. SE
Warren, OH 44484

Wooster ....
248 N. Walnut St.
Wooster, OH 44691

Youngstown ....
11 Central Sq. Suite 807
Youngstown, OH 44503

About the Author
David M. Chester, Attorney

David M. Chester has been an Ohio personal injury lawyer most of his legal career. After suffering a childhood injury at the hands of a careless driver, Attorney Chester understood the suffering that an injured victim endures. When he decided to become a lawyer, representing injured Ohioans was the obvious choice. From a single office, Attorney Chester has built a law firm with 20 offices located around the state of Ohio. His early life experience showed him that injured victims need compassion as well as competent, professional, aggressive representation. It is this philosophy that has defined Attorney Chester and brought him the success he currently enjoys.

Attorney Chester received his Bachelors degree in Business Pre-Law from Bowling Green State University. He obtained his Doctor of Jurisprudence from Cleveland State University College of Law, where he graduated 2nd in his law school class. After winning numerous law school awards, he finished in the top 3% on the Ohio Bar exam. He then moved from his home in Parma, Ohio south to Akron, Ohio where he established his main office.